S0-ACN-523

Aunt Netty and Me

Robert G. Wilson

Copyright © 2014 Robert G. Wilson

ISBN 978-1-63263-491-7

All rights reserved. No part of this publication may be reproduced, stored in a retrieval system, or transmitted in any form or by any means, electronic, mechanical, recording or otherwise, without the prior written permission of the author.

Published by BookLocker.com, Inc., Bradenton, Florida.

Printed in the United States of America on acid-free paper.

This is a work of historical fiction, based on actual persons and events. The author has taken creative liberty with many details to enhance the reader's experience.

BookLocker.com, Inc.
2014

Disclaimer

This memoir is my attempt to write the story of Clara's early life and is the result of her notes and my imagination about the five-six year span in which the tale unfolded. I tried, to the best of my ability, to retell events and conversations as truthfully as possible; in order to weave a creative story, however, it was necessary to invent (perhaps imperfectly) some dialogue and characters. It was certainly not my intention to harm anyone in the telling of this story.

Dedication

To Roberta, whose courage and cheerfulness echo that of Clara.

Acknowledgements

Without the help and encouragement of the following people this story would never have been told. The author appreciates the support of Tanya Rubinstein, Betsy Upton, Sybil Saam, Pat Jahoda, Bob Miles, Robb Thomson, Karen Wells, Candace Walsh, Ellen Kleinman, and Jane Wilson.

Table of Contents

Introduction 1

A Train to Newburyport 9

Getting Settled 13

The Big Party 21

Starting School 35

Letters from Mama 43

Where Is Home? 49

Mama Comes to Visit 63

Together Again 71

Dearie, do you remember when we
Waltzed to the Souza band
My wasn't the music grand
Chowder parties down by the seashore
Every Fourth of July, test your memory
My dearie
Do you recall when Henry Ford couldn't even fix
The running board under a Chandler six
Dearie, life was cheery
In the good old days gone by
Do you remember?

(Hilliard & Mann)

Introduction

There is a part of my early days I don't often talk about. It was a time of pain and it was a time of real happiness. There were people I feared, and others I learned to love deeply. But today, as I look back, I guess it was mostly a story of growing up. Here is part of that story.

· · · ·

When I was six we lived on Cypress Street in Watertown, Massachusetts. In those days Boston got its meat from the cattle in Watertown. The railroad from the west ran right through town. Our whole neighborhood smelled of the slaughterhouses, corrals and granaries nearby. Droves of cattle herded from the railroad often stopped the street trolley on North Beacon Street as the cattle bellowed and bleated into the Bleiler corrals.

The Bleilers were relatives of ours. Mama's sister, Elsie, married Ed Bleiler. They lived nearby, on the corner of School and Arsenal Streets. I knew the four Bleiler men, Ed, Frank, Charles, and Fred, all of them in the meat and butcher business. They also had a sister, Old Aunt Lizzie, whom we all liked. We called her "Granny." My papa was in the cattle business too, though he had started out planning to be a priest. Mama told me that as a boy he ran away from the seminary because he didn't like it. I asked Mama, "What was bad enough to make him run away? Didn't the seminary want him to stay?"

Later Mama told me the Bleilers had helped him get started in the cattle business.

Cypress Street and all the streets around us were dirt roads. In those days most folks didn't have automobiles, but we did have horses and buggies. I used to walk to the stable with Mama to help her curry the horse. Our buggy had a fringe all around the roof and I loved to watch it wave in the wind when we rode. In the winter we'd bundle up with big fur-lined robes when we went riding. I will never forget the musty smell of those robes when they got wet from the falling snow. They made me think of the old corncob pipes my Papa smoked. To cut down the dust on our dirt roads, now and again an oil wagon came through to sprinkle tar.

One day, Mama and I went to visit our neighbor, Mrs. Cheney. When we arrived she had just set my friend Sarah up on the sink-board in the kitchen and started counting her beautiful black curls. I felt awful as I watched. I had just had scarlet fever and my hair had been cut short, like a boy's because I had lost so much from the fever. At that moment, I hated Sarah and her hair. I fumed for weeks. Besides, Mama had dressed me in corduroy suits with buster-brown collars. I hated them. I thought they made me look even more like a boy. I didn't want to be a boy.

A few days later, Mrs. Cheney had her rugs airing out on the back clothesline, so I persuaded my little brother Ken to get a stick and put tar from the road on the rugs. Someone saw Ken do it, and reported it to Mama. Ken took the punishment but he never squealed. He was like that. His punishment meant that he could not go to the Lexington Battle Parade on April 19th. I had a miserable time and cried because I knew who should really be punished. But I was afraid to tell.

Dr. Nelligan was our doctor. I don't think he had an office. He just came to our house whenever we needed him. He came once when Ken had an abscess just forward of his ear. Dr. Nelligan put Ken on the ironing board and he chased me out of the room. Mama held Ken's head and Aunt Elsie had his feet, then the doctor just cut, no anesthetic. I can still hear poor Ken holler. It was scary, and I cried that time, too.

Another day, Dr. Nelligan came to the house because Bill had to have his tonsils out. In those days they performed minor surgery like that at home. Mama hurried us outdoors to play, but through the open windows we could hear Bill screaming, "Just one minute doctor, please, just wait one minute." Then Dr. Nelligan put the ether cap over Bill's nose and did the operation. Bill got his tonsils out in the kitchen while Mama assisted, and we listened!

Bill, my older brother, had a bad temper. One wintery day Bill had to stay indoors and take care of Ken and me while Mama went next door to see Mrs. Stewart. Bill wanted to go out and play in the snow. He sat at the dining room window getting madder and madder as he saw Mama and Mrs. Stewart talk in the kitchen across the lawn. Finally, in a terrific burst of temper, he smashed his hand on the window and broke the glass. Of course he cut his hand, but that didn't hurt as much as his punishment. The window had to be sealed with paper until the glazer came several days later, and Papa kept Bill in until it was fixed. That really made him mad! Sometimes Bill's temper scared me.

Winters must have been colder then. I can remember walking to school trying to get all the way there without breaking through the crust of the snow. I'd start off to school with Bill and some of his neighbor buddies. Mama told him to walk me to school. But somewhere along the way the boys ran ahead. By the time I trudged along, I'd get to school cold and crying, and late. The janitor, Mr. Coughlin, met me at the door and took me down to the boiler room where he put my mittens on the big drum of the furnace and rubbed my hands warm. Then he sent me upstairs to my classroom. Mama never knew why I got to school late so often.

While we lived on Cypress Street, Bill decided he wanted to try parachuting. He figured that he could go out the second story window with a bed-sheet. So he tied the corners together and hoisted himself out the window and went "plop," right to the ground. Fortunately, that time he hurt his pride, but not much else. That's how fearless Bill always acted. I admired his courage.

The back hall of our house on Cypress Street had an icebox. One of my chores as a girl was helping Mama empty the water pan under it. If I let the pan overflow, water flooded the back entry floor. Just off that entry, the pantry held two big barrels, one was for bread flour and the other for cake flour. I longed for the days when new barrels arrived. I always wanted to see them opened, because I had been told that I came in a flour barrel, so I always hoped I'd find a baby sister inside. Now and then Mama sent me down the cellar to bring up some apples, potatoes, or a dipper of the mincemeat kept in a big crock down there. Boy, did those apples and the mincemeat smell good!

Then one winter, Uncle Ed died. I must have been about seven. I didn't understand. Suddenly, when we went to visit Aunt Elsie, no Uncle Ed. Where had he gone? When would he come back? Mama tried to tell me, but she mostly cried. My older brother Bill didn't help me understand it, either.

And then, the next spring, Papa died. One day he came home from work sick. Then, for about two weeks, Dr. Nelligan and other men came to the house. And then Papa was gone too. I was eight. I don't remember much about the funeral, except that his casket filled our living room and many people came to look at him. When I reached in to hold his hand, it felt cold and it made me cry.

They buried Papa in a Catholic cemetery in Waltham. After his death, we all went down to Nantasket Beach for several days. During our stay in Nantasket, Dr. Nelligan had the house fumigated. It smelled like medicine when we came home.

After Papa died, Mama lost the house on Cypress Street because she couldn't keep up the payments. She told us that the priest who led Papa's funeral had borrowed money for the Church and never paid Papa back. And she also said that Papa had lost a lot of money when his partner cheated him on a big railroad shipment of calves from the west. I asked Mama. "What makes money so important?"

We all went to live with Old Aunt Lizzie on School Street. Both Mama and Aunt Elsie went to work at Hood Rubber Company making shoes and boots. I hated the way they smelled when they came home.

We lived with Aunt Lizzie for a year or more, I think I was in 3rd Grade, but she didn't like cooking and taking care of the boys. Bill and his cousins, Ernie and Roy, got into lots of trouble. At that time, I had a doll I loved. She had a china head, eyes that opened and closed, a sawdust body, but china hands and feet. Each year about Thanksgiving time, she would disappear. But at Christmas she'd be under the tree again with all new clothes. Oh, she was my greatest joy. One Christmas I got a doll carriage for her, and when I walked down the street, one of Aunt Elsie's neighbors said the carriage looked like a real baby carriage. I felt so proud. After Papa died and we moved to Auntie's house we stored her away in a trunk with other things. One day the boys found her in the trunk, put her up in the crotch of a tree and shot her full of bb shot. That day I really cried!

Ernie and Roy both grew up with their uncles, all cattlemen. So they and, of course, my brother Bill, all swore like sailors. They used cuss words like the King's English. Mama didn't want me to grow up that way, too. And she didn't want me to begin doing the same things the boys got into. So, when Aunt Lizzie starting taking in boarders, Mama decided we had to do something drastic. We had to be split up. That made me frightened and angry. I wanted to stay with Mama.

Ken, the youngest, went to Lexington to live with Grandma Kelly, one of Papa's relatives. My brother, Bill, the oldest, went to a farm in Plymouth, New Hampshire. Mama moved to New York City and got a job in a big clothing factory. I couldn't go with her. Instead, I was sent to Newburyport to live with an old family friend.

The day we left, Mama carried my things in a carpetbag but I clutched my new doll. We took the North Beacon Street trolley to the center of Watertown. There we transferred to a car that took us to Hay Market Square in Boston.

"I don't want to go, Mama."

"I know, Sissy. I don't want you to go either. But we must all be brave. We will get together again soon. I will write to you every week." I wondered if I would ever see my family again. I was very frightened and angry. I didn't want to be an orphan.

When we got off the trolley at Hay Market, a tall, thin lady all dressed in black met us. She wore a hat with a wide brim and she carried a rolled up black umbrella, even though it wasn't a rainy day.

Mama said, "Clara, this is Aunt Netty." I thought she must be very upset because she usually called me 'Sissy.' Mama and the lady spoke together for a few minutes, and then she took my things. But I held my dolly close. I tried not to cry, but when I saw Mama's eyes all red and teary, I couldn't help it. Mama hugged me hard and gave me a big kiss. Then the tall lady and I walked away to the railroad station. I felt scared and worried but I tried to be brave.

A Train to Newburyport

The train smelled smoky and hot. I couldn't sleep on the hard seats. The noise and rattle of the train shook me awake. The lady tried to tell me about the sights along the way, but I didn't pay much attention.

When we finally got to Newburyport, the sun had nearly set. A crippled man met us with a horse and carriage and drove us to a big house nearby. Later, I learned the crippled man was Mr. Munroe, who worked for Aunt Netty. At the house she took me to the kitchen where I had some milk and crackers. Then she carried my things up some wide stairs to a bedroom with a four-poster bed. She said, "This will be your room, and I will be right next door. You can call me if you need anything. Don't be afraid, dear. Everything will be all right." Then she helped me get ready for bed and put my doll in with me. She left a little light on by the door. The room and the bed smelled good, but I felt so very lonely. I think I cried a little. And I thought about how Papa had run away when he was a boy.

When I woke next morning the sun shone in the open window. I could hear birds singing outside. But I missed all the confusion of my brothers and I even missed Aunt Elsie's noisy boys. The house seemed too quiet. I didn't want to be here.

But I got dressed, and Aunt Netty showed me where to wash up in the bathroom right across the hall. Then we went downstairs to the big kitchen at the back of the house. She introduced me to her hired lady, Florence, who did all the cooking. Florence brought us a plate of eggs and bacon with fresh bread and honey. I guess I must have been hungry.

After breakfast, she showed me around the big house. Yesterday, all her clothes were black. Today, she dressed in all white. She wore a narrow skirt almost to the floor with white shoes that made her seem even taller and thinner. She had on a long white apron that had lace around the bottom. (It didn't look like an apron for working in the kitchen.) She swept her light red hair upward with a small clip holding it away from her neck. She wore glasses, but I noticed that she often wore them pushed up to the top of her head. I had never seen anyone do that before.

As she showed me the parlor and dining rooms she pointed out several paintings of her former husband. She quietly pointed out that he had died at sea, and showed me a picture of his ship. All the rooms seemed huge to me, and most had fireplaces. She showed me her favorite room, the library. It had a few big soft chairs and a huge desk with a green glass lamp on it. Books lined all the shelves. I had never seen so many books. In this room, a fireplace dominated the corner. Near it a window looked out on the garden.

At the back of the house, near the kitchen, she pointed out Florence's room. She instructed me never to go into that room unless Florence invited me. Aunt Netty said I could use almost any other room I wished, but that we usually used the parlor for guests. Then she said, "By the way, in a few weeks we are going to have some guests come in, so we'll have to get you some pretty new clothes. Would you like that?" I felt very out of place in such a fancy house, but the thought of new clothes made me feel better.

Next, we went out the back door to the garden. I felt more comfortable there. I recognized the flowering shrubs close to the house. I think she called them lilacs. She took some scissors from her apron and picked one to show me how sweet they smelled. I said, "They make me think of home. We had some like that by our kitchen door."

Big trees shaded most of the garden. One of them had a swing hanging from a thick old branch. As we walked along the path to the barn, she pointed out apple, pear, and peach trees and a high green hedge to break the wind. Near the big barn a flowerbed had been laid out in careful rows. She said that Mr. Munroe took care of the garden and lived in the barn. I could hardly believe she called it a barn. The big white building seemed only a little smaller than the house. It had two big doors facing the street and windows on both floors. Only it didn't have that little fenced in "lighthouse" thing the main house had. When I looked up at the main house I asked her about it. "That is called a widow's walk. Many of the houses had them so the captain's wives could see down to the Merrimack River and watch for the ships to sail in. I will take you up to see ours, but not today while I have clean clothes on. It's a little dusty up there."

Then she said, "Shall we cut some flowers for the table?" She again took the scissors from her apron pocket. She let me choose the flowers, and she cut a big bunch.

That night at supper we ate in the big dining room, just the two of us. The flowers we picked that morning decorated the table. It looked so pretty that I tried hard to be polite the way

Mama had taught me. She had a very soft voice. But I missed talking to my boisterous brothers, and I didn't know what to talk about. In one corner of the room stood a very tall clock with little steeples at the top. Every fifteen minutes, the bells played a tune, and every hour they rang out the time so loud that sometimes I had to listen hard to hear her talk. But this began a dinner ceremony that continued all the time I lived with Aunt Netty. She loved poetry and she loved reading aloud. After dessert, while she sipped coffee, she would read her favorite poems to me or to everyone at the table. Sometimes she asked me to read a poem after I finished dessert. If I stumbled on some of the words, she would gently help me, but she always wanted me to finish the whole poem. She had several poems, her favorites, which we read often. Sometimes she asked me what I thought the poem meant and we would talk about it. Sometimes she stopped to explain a word I didn't understand. But sometimes it was just a funny or nonsense poem, and we laughed together.

This first night she read a poem called "Luck" that she said had been written by a writer she knew, a woman named Abbie Farwell Brown. We read it often:

I sought a four-leaved clover, -
The grass was gemmed with dew, -
I searched the meadow over;
To find a four-leaved clover;
I was a lucky rover, -
You sought the charm-grass, too,
And seeking luck and clover
I found it – finding you.

Getting Settled

That night at bedtime she tucked my doll in with me and again read me a story before I went to sleep. The next day, before breakfast, she made me take a bath, in the morning. Mama had always had me I take my bath at the end of the day to shed the day's play dirt. And she said it in a funny way. It sounded like "ba-a-a-ath." But I relaxed in the warm water, and she put in some powder that made it smell good.

When I got out of the tub, I asked, "Yesterday you said there would be guests coming for a party. Will any of them be girls or boys?"

"No, I'm afraid not for this party, dear. These will be grown-ups, all friends of mine."

"Are there any boys or girls nearby for me to play with?"

"Yes, Clara, you will meet them when school opens again in the fall. Meanwhile, today we'd better get busy writing letters to your mother as we promised."

So after breakfast, she sat me down at the kitchen table with paper and pencils and she went off in the carriage with Mr. Munroe. Florence said, "She goes to the library every morning. She helps the librarian at the Newburyport Public Library on Milk Street."

It made me angry that she left me with only Florence, so I wrote a nasty letter saying how much I hated it here: no friends, nothing to do, and no one to play with.

After lunch she came home and read my letter. I had scribbled and scratched out a lot so I felt ashamed about the mean things I had written. She only said, "Let's write a nice neat copy, and I'll show you how to draw pictures in it for your Mom. I can understand how unhappy you are without your mother and brothers. When I am very blue, I often read poems. Would you like me to read a story or poem to you?"

So we went into her favorite room, the one with all the books, and we sat in one of the big soft chairs while she read me several poems. One of them, "Wynken, Blyken and Nod," I had heard before, but she read new ones too. I liked the way she read and I did feel a little better. Afterward she helped me write my letter again and together we drew pictures of stick people to show what we did yesterday.

That night for supper we ate again in the big dining room and it wasn't so bad. I guess I had gotten a little used to the clock and the poetry. We had apple pie for dessert and she asked me if I knew the poem about apple pie and cheese by Eugene Field. I didn't, so she read it.

"Apple-Pie and Cheese"
By Eugene Field

Full many a sinful notion
Conceived of foreign powers
Has come across the ocean
To harm this land of ours;
And heresies called fashions

Have modestly effaced,
And baleful, morbid passions
Corrupt our native taste
O tempora! O mores!
What profanations these
That seek to dim the glories
Of apple-pie and cheese!

Though ribald may decry 'em,
For these twin boons we stand,
Partaking thrice *per diem*
Of their fullness out of hand;
No enervating fashion
Shall cheat us of our right
To gratify our passion
With a mouthful at a bite!
We'll cut it square or bias,
Or any way we please,
And faith shall justify us
When we carve our pie and cheese!

After a big piece of apple pie, she helped me into bed, read me the rest of the poem, and then left some books for me to read before I went to sleep.

For the next several days time went much the same way, breakfast, then Aunt Netty went to the library, I played in the garden until lunch, then she would read to me or show me around the house. During that time, I got to be good friends with Florence and Mr. Munroe and his horse. Though Mr. Munroe limped badly, he helped me a lot. When I felt blue he told me stories. We became friends. He always called me "Miss Clara."

Then one day, Aunt Netty asked if we'd like to go on a picnic on Saturday. Mr. Munroe got out the buggy and took us to Atkinson Park, way out on High Street. We went wading, had a picnic of sandwiches, cool drinks and fresh plums, and I even met some other girls. In my next letter to Mama, I had a lot more things to draw stick figures doing. I even drew Benny the horse.

On Sunday I went to church with Aunt Netty for the first time. She helped me lay out my best clothes and after a bath she brushed and combed my hair and tied it with a big white bow. Florence had starched and ironed the pleats in my white blouse and I thought it looked extra pretty. Mr. Munroe rigged up the carriage and took us down Federal Street to the church where many carriages milled around.

As we rode, Aunt Netty said, "I'd like you to meet some of my friends at church. Today there is no special service for the children, so you can sit with me. But in a few weeks Sunday school will begin again, and then you can meet some other children from the church."

I had never seen a bigger church. A tall white steeple towered over the entrance and a loud bell rang as we rode up. Everyone seemed to know Aunt Netty. People came over to greet us as we walked to the door, and she introduced me to many of them before we went in. Inside didn't look like our old church in Watertown at all. It looked very sunny and white, but it had no colored windows or crosses around like ours, Some people sat in the balconies on both sides of the church.

A man led us down the center aisle to show us where to sit. But instead of long wooden benches on each side, this church had small booths with a white wooden door on each. He took us to one of the booths way up front that had a little metal plaque on it. And the benches had cushions for us to sit on. He closed the door to the booth after we sat down. When I turned around I could see the choir and a big organ on another balcony at the back of the church over the entrance door. I also noticed a tall white-haired gentleman in the booth across the aisle from us. I think he knew us, because he kept looking at Aunt Netty and me.

The service bored me, and the room felt sweaty and hot. But I liked the music because I knew some of the hymns. The high booths meant I couldn't see many of the other people, except those in the balconies. After the service, the tall man across the aisle came over to say hello, and Aunt Netty introduced me.

She said, "Clara, this is Captain Cross. I'm sure he'd like to meet you." He patted my head, but we didn't have a chance to talk because of all the people in the aisle.

Aunt Netty introduced me to more people, including some children, but I didn't remember many names. I did notice that everyone dressed beautifully, especially the other girls. I also noticed that many people when they spoke to Aunt Netty said things like, "Congratulations," and "How happy you must be." I wondered what they meant. People treated me like an old friend, and I felt good next to Aunt Netty even though I didn't know them.

Mr. Munroe met us outside the church, and by the time we got home my good clothes felt very messy and wrinkled. Aunt Netty said, "Tomorrow, instead of going to the library, I think we will go shopping downtown. We will look for some new clothes. You will need some school clothes, and perhaps we can find a pretty party dress for you. Would you like that?" That sounded like great fun to me. Maybe I could like it here after all!

At dinner that night she read me another poem by Eugene Field. She liked to read from her favorite women poets like Abbie Farwell Brown, Sara Teasdale, or Emily Dickinson, but she said that Field was usually a lot funnier. So she read a story about a little boy named Tim called "The Ballad of the Jelly-Cake."

> A little boy whose name was Tim
> Once ate some jelly-cake for tea –
> Which cake did not agree with him,
> As by the sequel you shall see
> 'My darling child,' his mother said,
> For, after you have gone to bed,
> I fear 't will make your stomach ache!'
> But foolish little Tim demurred
> Unto his mother's warning word.
>
> That night, while all the household slept,
> Tim felt an awful pain, and then
> From out the dark a nightmare leapt
> And stood upon his abdomen!
> 'I cannot breathe!' the infant cried –
> 'Oh Mrs. Nightmare, pity take!'
> 'There is no mercy,' she replied,
> 'For boys who feast on jelly-cake!'
> And so, despite the moans of Tim,
> The cruel nightmare went for him.

The poem went on and on, but wasn't scary. I enjoyed it. We laughed, and I didn't have any nightmares.

The Big Party

On Monday, as she promised, Aunt Netty didn't go to the library. Instead Mr. Munroe got out the carriage and took us to a store named Seligmann's on Lime Street. He left us at the store and said he would wait with the carriage just down the street. As we went in, I noticed a beautiful party dress in the window.

The storeowner seemed to know Aunt Netty and greeted her warmly as she began showing us school clothes. At first she brought out cotton pleated dresses like I had worn at home in Watertown. They looked nice to me, but Aunt Netty seemed to want some frillier things. So we picked out two really pretty skirts with embroidery and ruffles, as well as a tan jumper dress with some new white blouses. A few of the things didn't fit quite right, but Mrs. Seligmann said she had a lady who would do the alterations. That surprised me, because at home Mama had always done the alterations herself while I stood covered with pins.

Then Aunt Netty asked about the party dress in the window. Mrs. Seligmann brought it in so I could try it on. It was a beautiful soft white silk with embroidery around the neck and it came with a matching sun hat decorated with ribbons and flowers. But what a disappointment. The store only had the dress in one size, and it was obviously too long. Mrs. Seligmann must have seen my face fall, so she suggested that while her alterations lady, Mrs. Uloth, made adjustments to the school clothes, perhaps she could shorten and fix the dress at the same time. She and Aunt Netty talked for a while and then asked whether I would like that. Of course that thrilled me and we all agreed.

About that time, into the store came the tall man we met at church on Sunday, Captain Cross. He said, "I saw Munroe and your carriage down the street. I knew where you'd be." He turned to me and said, "How are you, Clara? Finding school clothes? When do classes start?"

"Yes, sir. And a party dress too. School starts pretty soon, I think."

"Netty, you'll spoil the child."

"No. I think not. We are having a party next week, and I'd hate to have her feel shabby."

"Thanks for inviting me. Yes, I'll be there. Clara, let's you and I talk again. I want to know more about your family. You must miss them."

"Yes, sir. I especially miss my brothers."

Then he turned and left without saying goodbye.

We picked out some white stockings and looked at a woolen red short-sleeved bathing suit, but decided to wait on that. Soon Mr. Munroe picked us up and we trotted home.

Preparations for the party began on a Thursday. Aunt Netty hired another girl to help Florence with the cooking and cleaning. Florence enjoyed having someone else to order around. Netty also hired a waiter and waitress to serve at dinner, but they would not come until the next day. Meanwhile, we all pitched in. Florence brought out the good silver and glasses and showed me how they needed to be polished. We opened the big table in the dining room and Munroe helped us with the extra leaf and the spare chairs. With all the extra work getting ready for the party, Florence asked if I would mind helping her make the beds. She said, "I know Mrs. Cross doesn't want you doing housework, but I think even rich girls should know how to make beds." So Florence and I went upstairs and she showed me how to make hospital corners as we changed the sheets on Aunt Netty's bed. We got to be good at doing it, and we became good friends. Later, she asked me to write a note for the iceman asking him to leave an extra big block of ice next morning. I don't think she knew how to write very well. But she was a good cook. By suppertime the kitchen smelled wonderfully of pies, pastries and spices. We all hummed with excitement.

On Friday morning, Aunt Netty and I picked big bunches of flowers from the garden and made several arrangements for tables around the house. The she asked if I would help by setting the dinner table. I was thrilled to perform that very adult task. She set one place as an example, the turned me loose with the good silver, antique china and assorted mysterious glassware. I worked hard to follow her exacting pattern precisely, matching the position of each spoon and wine glass carefully. When I finished, she gave her approval with almost no corrections, and explained why each piece held that particular spot.

We planned for twelve people. So we discussed the delicate task of place cards and who should sit where. I felt very grown-up.

Later in the day the hired waiter and waitress came and we checked their uniforms.

That's how I learned two interesting things. When the waiter arrived he said, "Good afternoon, Mrs. Cross." I seldom heard Aunt Netty called "Mrs. Cross." And when I looked at the place cards on the dining room table I saw one for "Captain Cross." I began to guess that the white haired gentleman from church on Sunday must be a relative.

I asked her about it as she helped me with my bath and as she brushed my hair. She said, "Yes, Captain Cross is my father-in-law. He is my late husband's father. They both came from a long line of ship captains and ship builders. The Cross family started building ships here in Newburyport before the Revolutionary War. If you wish, sometime I'll show you a book about their history. You will find it interesting. By the way, Captain Cross may want to speak with you this evening. He would like to know you better."

Then she helped me with the new party dress from Seligmann's. I giggled with excitement.

Just before the big clock in the dining room struck seven, people began to arrive. Most came into our driveway in carriages, which Munroe led over to our barn. He had plenty of places for the horses there.

But suddenly we heard a big strange noise and up rode an automobile! I had only seen one or two before and never up close. The driver up front wore a hat and goggles and who should get out of the back but the tall white-haired gentleman, Captain Cross. He wore a long white coat that he handed to the waiter as he came in our front door. He said,

"Good evening, Clara. You are looking lovely this evening."
I think I blushed.

As Aunt Netty greeted everyone at the door she introduced
me to them and I tried to guess who went with each of the
place cards in the dining room. I met Miss Atkinson, the
schoolteacher, who arrived alone, and Dr. and Mrs. Tyng,
who came in a closed carriage. Next came Judge and Mrs.
Moseley (she was very fat!). Then Aunt Netty took
particular care to introduce me to Mr. and Mrs. Greenleaf
because of their connections to the Newburyport Library on
Milk Street. She said she hoped that I would get to know
Mrs. Greenleaf a lot better.

Reverend and Mrs. Tracey arrived last. I recognized the
minister from the church on Sunday. Mrs. Tracey looked
younger and even taller than he, and she was very beautiful.

In fact, as they filed into the parlor the beautiful clothes of
both the men and women impressed me. The women wore
long shimmery dresses decorated with lace and jewels or
pearls. A few wore elegant hats with feathers or flowers that
they left in our entrance hallway. I began to realize that Aunt
Netty must be an important person in Newburyport. I
wondered if I belonged.

Soon the waiter circulated with trays of cool drinks for the
ladies and wine for the gentlemen. The waitress followed
with little snacks that Florence had made that morning. Since
everyone seemed to know one another I heard lots of noisy
conversation and laughter. I sat next to Miss Atkinson, the
teacher, who of course wanted to know about the schools I
had attended. I tried to be polite, but I mostly wanted to
listen to the others talking.

Then Captain Cross came to my rescue. He said, "Before dinner begins, I'd like to talk with you. Perhaps Miss Atkinson would excuse us if we went into the library."

I didn't know what to expect, but followed him down the hall. Netty watched us go.

In the library, I sat in one of the big soft chairs near the fireplace but Captain Cross just walked slowly back and forth across the room. He said, "Clara, tell me about your home. I understand you lived in Watertown. What does your father do?"

"My Papa died last year."

"Oh, that's too bad. What work did he do?"

"Papa was a butcher. He and Uncle Ed worked together."

"That's a hard trade. Did they do well?"

"I guess so. I liked our big house on Cypress Street. But we had to move in with Old Aunt Lizzie when Papa died."

"Tell me about Aunt Lizzie?"

"Her name was Bleiler. The Bleilers owned the corrals on the corner of Arsenal Street."

"Did you like living with Aunt Lizzie?"

"I didn't mind. But Mama decided we had to move. She went to New York looking for work."

"Do you write to Mama?"

"Yes, sir. Aunt Netty helps me write a letter every few days."

"And does your Mama write to you?"

"Yes, sir. I got a letter just yesterday. She found a good job in a clothing factory in New York. She hopes we can move in with her again soon."

As he paced across the room he said, "That would be nice. You said the other day that you had brothers. Where are they?"

"Kenny lives with Granma Kelly in Lexington. He's only eight. My older brother, Bill, lives on a farm in New Hampshire. He's 13 and helps with the animals there."

"And you were sent to live here. Do you like living with Netty?"

"Yes, sir. She is very good to me. But I wish there were more children. I miss my brothers."

"And what about Munroe? Is he good to you? You know, I understand he knew some of the Bleilers in Boston. Did you know that?"

"No, sir. He never told me that. Mr. Munroe is very good to me. He tells me stories to make me feel better."

"Aye, Munroe is a good story-teller, he is. Well, we'd best drift into the dining room. I guess Netty must have dinner ready for us. Thank you for talking with me, Clara. I learned a lot."

I enjoyed the dinner, at least most of it. I sat near Aunt Netty on one side of the long table next to Mrs. Greenleaf from the library. I didn't mind talking with her. She invited me to spend a day at the library with her. I liked the dinner too, although I had never had roast duck before.

I watched the mysterious wine glasses at each place. Most of the ladies had white wine, so the waiter removed the other big glass. Reverend Tracey didn't have any wine, so the waiter took away both wine glasses. But Captain Cross and Aunt Netty had red wine. I watched as Captain Cross took a few sips, then looked at his glass for a long time as he swirled the wine around and around. He seemed to be thinking. When he looked up and saw me watching, he smiled in a funny way.

Everyone seemed to enjoy the party, but trouble started when the waiter and waitress started serving dessert. About this time, the big clock began striking 10:00, and Captain Cross, sitting on the other side of the table said, " Clara, I think it is time you go to bed." He said it with an angry scowl, so I hung my head and started to push back my chair. The room got quiet as everyone waited to see what would happen next. Aunt Netty reached over and touched my arm before I could get up from the table as she said, "Tomorrow is not a school day, and I'm sure Clara would not mind staying up for dessert with our guests."

The Captain seemed to stiffen in his chair as he said, "In my household children are in bed by 8:00, not gallivanting around in fancy parties until midnight. She will soon be sick."

Aunt Netty straightened herself, and looking right at the Captain replied, "Captain Cross, this is my household and I will see to it that Clara remains healthy even if she stays up late once in a while. Clara, would you like some dessert?"

"Yes, ma'am." At this, Captain Cross harrumphed and got up from the table. A few minutes later we heard his automobile rumble down the driveway. Conversation at the table started up again, even a bit noisier than before.

I'm glad I stayed. The dessert was strawberry shortcake! I felt good that Aunt Netty stood up for me. It made me wonder whether Captain Cross liked me.

Everyone knew of Netty's tradition of reading poetry with dessert and coffee, so they waited with expectation for what she chose for tonight. Netty did not disappoint. She remarked that one of her favorite poets, Abbie Farwell Brown, had made a visit to Newburyport on a speaking tour, and that tonight we were privileged to hear one of her latest works. She said, "It is called *The Cross-Current* and it seems especially appropriate for me to read it."

"The Cross-Current"
by A. F. Brown

> "Through twelve stout generations
> New England blood I boast;
> The stubborn pastures bred them,
> The grim, uncordial coast,

Sedate and proud old cities, -
Loved well enough by me,
Then how should I be yearning
To scour the earth and sea.

Each of my Yankee forbears
Wed a New England mate:
They dwelt and did and died here,
Nor glimpsed a rosier fate.

My clan endured their kindred;
But foreigners they loathed,
And wandering folk, and minstrels,
And gypsies motely-clothed.

Then why do patches please me,
Fantastic, wild array?
Why have I vagrant fancies
For lads from far away.

My folk were godly Churchmen, -
Or paced in Elders' weeds;
But all were grave and pious
And hated heathen creeds.

Then why are Thor and Wotan
To dread forces still?
Why does my heart go questing
For Pan beyond the hill?

My people clutched at freedom. –
Though others' wills they chained, -
But made the Law and kept it, -
And Beauty, they restrained.

Then why am I a rebel
To laws of rule and square?
Why would I dream and dally,
Or, reckless, do and dare?

O righteous, solemn Grandsires,
O dames, correct and mild,
Who bred me of your virtues!
Whence comes this changing child? –

The thirteenth generation, -
Unlucky number this! –
My grandma loved a Pirate,
And all my faults are his!

A gallant, ruffled rover,
With beauty-loving eye,
He swept Colonial waters
Of coarser, bloodier fry.

He waved his hat to danger,
At Law he shook his fist.
Ah, merrily he plundered,
He sang and fought and kissed!

Though none have found his treasure,
And none his part would take, -
I bless that thirteenth lady
Who close him for my sake!

There was a very hearty round of applause and vigorous conversation before everyone thanked Netty for the evening and gradually drifted toward home.

After breakfast the next morning, Netty asked, "Did you enjoy the dinner yesterday? Everyone commented on how pretty you looked and how well you handled yourself with all the adults. I am very proud of you."

"Yes, I had fun. Everyone was very nice to me, and they enjoyed the party and the poem you read. It caused a lot of conversation, but I didn't really understand it. Are you, like the lady who wrote the poem, really a 12th or 13th generation New Englander? How far back does that go? And I didn't understand the part about the pirate. Did your grandma really marry a pirate?"

She chuckled. "No, Clara, my grandmother didn't marry a pirate. But I think Abbie Brown's grandma probably did. She is from a very old New England family that lived in Boston. But she was a bit of a rule breaker. I admire people like that, and I guess I'm a bit of a nonconformist and Bohemian myself. But, more important, I think more people in this dusty old town should be like that, question the rules, stand on your own, and live for the beauty in life. That's what I wanted people to hear and to think about. It is something I'd like you to think about too. You are not too young to learn to think for yourself and to stand up for the beauty and justice in life."

"Is that why you argued with Captain Cross, too? He seemed very angry."

"Yes, exactly. He may be a Captain, but he doesn't set the rules in my house. And yes, I guess he was angry. But don't let that bother you. Everyone knows he gets that way sometimes. He wasn't angry with you. I'll tell you more about him. Meanwhile, I'd like to hear about your conversation with him before dinner. Let's go into the library."

So we went into her favorite room and sat in the big chairs by the window looking out on the garden.

She said. "Tell me about your talk with Captain Cross. What did he ask you?"

"He wanted to know about my home in Watertown and about Papa and Uncle Ed. He asked about Mama and whether she wrote to me. He asked whether I liked living with you."

"And what did you tell him?"

"Oh, I told him I like living here very much and that you treated me fine, but that I missed my brothers. And I told him I hoped for more children to play with. Then I told him about the letters we wrote to Mama. He also asked about Mr. Munroe. He said that Munroe knew some of Uncle Ed's brothers in Boston. I didn't know that."

"I'll tell you a story about that. You see, years ago, Mr. Munroe sailed on my husband's ship. On one of their trips to Nova Scotia, Munroe fell and had a bad accident. After that he couldn't sail anymore and had a hard time making a living. When he got really desperate he drifted down to Boston and took a terribly dirty job in one of the cattle yards owned by your uncles, the Bleiler brothers. Captain Cross always thought Munroe should have stayed here in Newburyport where his own family could have helped him. It took me a long time to locate Munroe, and finally I brought him back home, not Captain Cross. He always seemed to resent that I gave Munroe a job. He didn't think we should interfere with Munroe's class of people."

"What do you mean by 'Munroe's class of people?"

"Well, Captain Cross never got over the fact that Munroe was only a common seaman on one of his ships, not an educated man like him. In his eyes, that makes him feel superior."

"Did he ask what you thought about Munroe?"

"Yes ma'am. I told him what a good story teller Mr. Munroe is and how much I like talking with him."

"Good, Clara. I think you handled yourself very well. You know, Captain Cross often likes to boss people around. We mustn't let him do that to us. You noticed last evening how he tried to set the rules for you in my house. I can't let him do that."

"Thank you, I really liked the strawberry shortcake."

"I thought you would. But for me it meant more than just the dessert. Do you remember the poems we read the other day by that lady Abbie Farwell Brown? She wrote those poems about the Indian Pipes and the long one I read last night called *The Cross Current*? Well, I am very fond of her poems and stories, so next week I'd like you to come with me to the library so you can learn more about her background and education. She is quite a woman. Abbie Farwell Brown is also someone that would have let you stay up for dessert. She is a good friend of mine. I'd like you to know her. On Monday, let's both go to the library."

Starting School

About two weeks later, school started. The trip to the library with Netty had been fun, and, even though I hadn't met Abbie Farwell Brown herself as I expected, I did get to know more about her from Mrs. Greenleaf, the librarian.

The day before school opened, Netty had Mr. Munroe drive us to the school so she could introduce me to my new 4th grade teacher. The school sat a few blocks down the hill near the big white church we went to on Federal Street.

While we drove, Aunt Netty told me the story of how Captain Cross' grandfather had given the land for the school to the town back before the Revolutionary War. When we arrived, Miss Atkinson greeted us, but she wasn't my teacher. She had the older children in grades 5-8.

Miss Blodgett introduced herself. She taught 3rd and 4th grades. She asked me a few questions to be certain I qualified for 4th grade. When I told her about the books I read and the poems we read at dinner she seemed satisfied, so showed me to her classroom.

The school only held a few rooms. Her class met in a nice, white, sunny room on the ground floor. Five sets of school-desks lined each side of a wide aisle that led to the front of the room. Her plain wooden table and chair stood underneath a big blackboard with the alphabet printed in white letters across the top. To the right of her desk, two windows streamed sunlight across the room. Between the two windows stood an iron stove with a black chimney pipe that went up through the ceiling. On the left side, near the front was another window and beside it an upright piano. (I had never seen a schoolroom with a piano!) High shelves filled with books lined either side of the blackboard. A big globe of the world sat on a stand in the corner to the right of Miss Blodgett's desk. There was a flag in the corner and pictures of George Washington on the walls.

The desks looked just like the ones at our school in Watertown, except they were wide enough to hold two people. The back of each seat attached to the desk behind. Each desk had a hole for an inkwell and the top hinged over a compartment to store pencils, paper, and books. I liked the school. It felt very much like ours at home.

Miss Blodgett then told me about school hours, showed me where the children usually ate their lunch, and told me about some of the other children who would be in class with me. Outside, the schoolyard had a few tables and benches, a May pole, and two swings hanging from trees nearby.

The next day, Tuesday, I got up early. After I had a bath, I put on my new school clothes and ran downstairs even before Florence had breakfast ready. Aunt Netty packed a lunch for me, and instead of going to the library, said she would walk me to school the first day. We started down Federal Street while I clutched my new pencil case, a new school notebook and my lunch bag. It was an easy five-block walk down the hill. Along the way, we saw other children also heading to school. Just after we passed Prospect Street we met Margie, one of the girls Miss Blodgett said would be in my class. I was glad to see she lived close to our house on High Street.

Aunt Netty left me at the school door and I headed into my new classroom. Miss Blodgett acted a lot sterner than yesterday, but she tried to calm me down as she showed me where to sit. My desk was second from the front on the right and next to the window. Margie sat right behind me.

Soon the room filled with children and I understood why the seats were so wide. Across the aisle two boys shared a desk and behind me two girls sat together. Outside somewhere a bell rang, and Miss Blodgett rose from her desk and said, "All right, boys and girls. We will start the day." She moved to the piano, but before she sat down she said, "Today we will sing 'My Country 'Tis of Thee'. Before the season is over I want you to know all the verses. Today we will sing verses One and Two." Then she played and the class sang –

Fortunately I knew the words to the first verse pretty well, but I had to mumble through the second. I hoped she didn't notice.

Then she announced that arithmetic would be the first lesson of the day. She asked the boy in front of me to hand out books of multiplication tables from the shelf next to the blackboard. Since this was 4th grade, everyone should know the tables up through the nines, but for review she began the class on the fives. The entire class started reciting the fives table out loud as Miss Blodgett tapped her pointer to keep time. It bored me, but I guess I needed the review. At the end, she called on a few of the girls to write answers to a few problems on the board. I'm glad she didn't call on me.

Next came an hour of reading. This time she asked one of the girls across the aisle to hand out poetry books to everyone. Miss Blodgett selected "The Village Blacksmith" for us to read. She began on my side of the room and each of us in turn had to read part of a stanza out loud. My throat felt dry, so I read nervously and tripped on a few words that made the rest of the class laugh. But I guess I did all right.

At lunchtime, everyone jumped up and ran outdoors. I took a seat at one of the picnic tables and ate the lunch Aunt Netty had packed while all the other children ran or played games. After a while Margie came over to sit with me when she saw I was alone. We talked about our families and got to know one another. I learned that Margie's name was Uloth, and that her mother did the alterations at Seligmann's. I liked Margie.

After lunch my troubles really began. Miss Blodgett asked us to do a writing exercise in our school notebooks. As she walked around the room watching each of us, she stopped at my desk and said, "Clara, you are 4th grade now. You must start learning to write with your right hand. In this school no one writes with their left."

I heard the boy across the aisle giggle at what she said.

I got very red in the face. I had always been left-handed. I didn't know how to hold the pencil any other way.

At the end of the day, as Margie and I left school, one of the boys, I think his name was Billy, ran past us and shouted, "So long, Lefty!"

Maybe he thought that was funny. I didn't. I began to cry again.

Then I got a surprise. On the other side of School Street, I saw Munroe sitting in his buggy! Bundles filled the back of the wagon but he waved as he shouted, "Climb aboard. I'll give you a lift up the hill."

Margie and I hopped up on the box seat with Munroe and we trotted off. He could see I was crying, but didn't say anything until Margie jumped off at Prospect Street. Then we rode right up to our house and into the barn. After we unloaded the wagon and unhitched the horses, Munroe said, "Somehow I reckoned the first couple days might be stormy for you. That's why I drifted by onto School Street today. Now, what brought on those tears?"

So I told him how the teacher had made me write with the other hand, and how awful I felt when the boy called me, 'Lefty'.

Munroe said, "Well now, Miss Clara, that ain't such a bad nickname. I've heard worse. Why, I sailed with a mate we called Lefty and I never saw a man who could splice a line faster than he could. He just made that marlinspike fairly fly. And then I knew a left-handed dragger in Nova Scotia who could open oysters and scallops faster than any man I ever met. Being good with the left hand ain't so bad."

"Yes, but Miss Blodgett won't let me *use* my left hand. I can't even hold the pencil right!" I was still furious.

"Well, I'd say, let's get you to gibe around and show her how smart you can sail on the starboard tack. I'll show *you* how to hold your pencil, and you show *me* how neat you can make them letters. Then I'll bet the two of us can show *her* who is skipper of this ship."

So, for the next few weeks, every afternoon after school, Munroe and I worked at learning to write and print with my right hand. It didn't always work, so sometimes in class I'd forget and pick up the pencil in the left hand. Whenever she saw me, Miss Blodgett slashed me on my wrist with a switch she always had close by. Not only did it hurt, but also I felt childish. I hung my head. I was sure the class thought I was such a dope! But I gritted my teeth and learned not to cry.

Then a funny thing began to happen. Almost every time she stung my wrist with her switch, I noticed other children in the room would wince or squeal. And one day, at lunch, one of the girls, Lenore, came over and gave me a little cupcake her Mom had made, and said how sorry she was about my troubles. Another time, Billy came by and said, "Hey, Lefty. Don't let her get the best of you. We're all with you."

And funny, the more she leaned on me, the madder I got, the harder I worked, both with Munroe and on my schoolwork. One day I got a letter from Mama. When I read it to Munroe he noticed that she always called me Sissy. Munroe said, "We're getting to be shipmates, so I can't keep calling you 'Miss Clara' like you wuz the lady of the house. And, I can't call you 'Sissy' like your Ma does. But I notice no matter how stormy things be, you are always a mite sunny. So I'm a mind to call you 'Sunny'. Is that shipshape with you?"

"That's shipshape, with me. It's sure better than calling me 'Miss Clara.' We both laughed.

So from that time on the name stuck, and everyone, except Aunt Netty, called me Sunny. She always called me Clara, even when she wasn't cross.

The funny things is, I had never told her about the switch, and Munroe never told her either. But somehow Aunt Netty heard about my troubles with Miss Blodgett. Maybe she learned through her friend Miss Atkinson. But in some way she began to guess.

One day after school she called me into her library and said, "Clara, show me your arms please."

The day before had been a bad day, and Miss Blodgett had hit me with her switch. My left wrist was still sore and showed red marks. Netty ran her fingers gently over my wrist and then got very red in the face. "How did this happen, dear" she asked.

I didn't want to tell her, but it was a relief that Munroe and I would no longer hold the secret alone anymore. I not only told her about the switch and the welts, but I cried as I told about how miserable it made me feel with the rest of the kids. I also told her about how some of them used to call me, Lefty, but how things had changed a little now. And I told her about the help that Munroe had given me. When I finished I think we were both crying. She gave me a big hug just like Mama used to as she said, "Clara, she will never hit you again, I promise. I will see to that."

The next day was a Wednesday and she said, "Clara, you may stay home from school today. You may use the desk in my library to study and read. I want Munroe to take me down to school. In fact, instead of going to school, why don't you spend the time writing a letter to your Mama."

That afternoon, when she came home Netty said, "If that teacher ever strikes you again for any reason I want you to be certain to tell me. It *is* school policy that you learn to write with your right hand, but I will *not* stand for cruelty or physical punishment. I understand that you do very well in school, even with your right hand. I will not let that woman break your spirit with her ancient, backward ways. Munroe tells me how hard you have worked to prevent that. I am very proud of you, and I love you very much. You are very special to me."

Then she hugged me and we went together to have some milk and cookies. I showed her the letter I had written to Mama, and she didn't even ask me to copy it over. I had written it right-handed.

For the rest of 4th grade, Miss Blodgett never hit me again and I never saw her switch again, even when I sometimes slipped and picked up my pencil with the "wrong" hand.

But everyone noticed how often I seemed to get the toughest words to spell, and the most difficult arithmetic problems at the blackboard. Miss Blodgett always seemed to take a special interest in me. But as this continued to make some classmates sympathize with me, it helped me make friends with a lot more children in Miss Blodgett's class.

As I think back on it, I'm almost glad. It helped me make some really good friends, and I also learned to write with both hands!

Letters from Mama

Two weeks before Christmas, we had a big snowstorm on a Thursday and Friday, so school closed. Snow drifted deep around all the doors. Someone rigged a big roller that a team of horses dragged along the roads to tamp down the drifts. Munroe hitched our horses to an open sleigh so we could get around town, but not everyone was so lucky. Many people had no choice but to trudge through the deep snow.

For me, it meant lots of fun. The hill in back of our house ran down to Low Street and made a wonderful place for sliding. My classmates, Margie and Billy, hiked over from their houses with sleds, and we spent the afternoon with the other kids in the snow. Afterward, Florence made hot chocolate and cookies, but when she saw Billy, she said, "Isn't that the fishmonger's son? I hope you don't play with him often. I buy fish in his shop, and I wouldn't want him to think he could be a regular visitor in your home. You ought to have better friends than him."

I told her that I liked Billy, and that he was a good friend of mine from school.

Every day until Christmas got more exciting. Netty had Munroe take us out into the country on the sleigh where we cut a big Christmas tree and loads of greens for decorations. The sleigh had bells and even had a warm, heavy robe that smelled just like the one in our sleigh at home. Almost every evening we had a fire in one of the fireplaces. That made the house smell good and cozy. Netty got out of storage piles of

Christmas ribbons, candles, and special dishware, while Florence kept busy making cakes, cookies and other treats. No one talked about presents, but Munroe took many mysterious trips to town.

Netty planned to invite friends to the house for Christmas Eve. This time she also invited some of my friends and their parents, so it would be fun for me too. She included Mr. and Mrs. Uloth, Margie's parents, and Billy's father, Mr. Boudreaux, from the fish market, though Florence didn't seem to like serving him. Every night at supper, instead of reading poems, we read chapters of *A Christmas Carol*. And she also found a Christmas story by her friend Abbie Brown.

About this time, while we were having fun getting ready for the holiday, I got another letter from Mama. Here's the one I saved from about that time:

Dear Sissy,

I was so happy getting your letter. I'm glad you are liking school better. You was always good at school. You ought to keep it up good.

Work here is good but hard. I leave house early when it's dark and dark when I get home. But they make me floor lady now so I don't sew I supervise the other girls. This is different kind of work. Some are not hard worker like me and I have to stay after them. Just like when Mr. Bezak the plumber used to loaf on the job. And I always must see that bundles are always ready for the fast girls or they get angry. But I like it better.

It gets cold weather here and my apartment is small. I hope maybe soon I get better job and better apartment so you can come live again as family. My heart aches with you so far away. Billie doesn't write much, but says he likes the farm. His school stays closed lots because of heavy snow. He always says "Hello" to you.

You do what Aunt Netty says and tell her thanks for taking good care of you. I bet you're getting to be big girl. I miss you lots.

Love,

Mama

It made me sad to think we weren't together. It sounded like New York wasn't much fun for her. I wished we could all be together again soon. I could hardly remember what they all looked like. It made me gloomy, despite the season.

Just before that Christmas, we had another terrific big, heavy snowstorm. All the roads were deep in snow, and school closed early. Several of the farmers nearby brought out teams of horses again, pulling those big rollers to tamp down the snow on the main streets. Mr. Munroe got our horse-drawn sleigh out of the barn. At Christmas time he rigged the sleigh with chains of bells that made wonderful music as the horse trotted along. Aunt Netty set up our beautiful tree by the window in the parlor, while Florence baked her special Christmas cookies and candies. She taught me how to decorate them with stars, trees and wreaths. This was the start of a really good friendship with Florence. I said to her, "This is the most fun I ever had at Christmas."

But finally, Christmas Eve arrived with the big party. All the rooms were decked with candles, decorations and greenery. The big tree in the parlor sparkled with crystal hangings and a shiny star at the very top. A big punch bowl on the dining room table sat surrounded by little cakes and treats. As people came in, many carried bottles of wine or presents (even a few for me!). Captain Cross brought a cheerful greeting, "Merry Christmas, Sunny." Even he had a present for me, but he left his fancy car at home because of the snow. People wandered around the house visiting and talking, until late in the evening, everyone collected in the parlor to sing carols around the tree.

Then the most amazing thing happened. As the guests went out into the cold to go home, the sky filled with beautiful bands of green, yellow, and red, the Northern Lights. I had never seen them before. We all stood shivering in the cold and watched the display but could not turn away. This was the first Christmas I spent away from Mama and my family. I wondered if Mama could see these lights over the big buildings of New York. Again, it made me sad to think we were not together.

The next morning, I jumped out of bed early to run downstairs. There piled under the tree were heaps of packages large and small. At first I looked around for my favorite doll. Mama had always given her a new set of clothes in time for Christmas. Then I saw under the tree a whole new doll fresh from Seligmann's window downtown and I stopped fretting. It was the most beautiful doll I had ever seen. She had blonde, curly hair, real shoes you could take off, and a beautiful, fluffy pink dress covered by a red velvet cape. And when I picked her up, her voice said,

"Mama." I knew I would be the envy of all the girls in my class.

There were packages for everyone, including Florence and Munroe. Florence helped me make a traditional spicy Irish Christmas cake crammed with fruit and nuts, that we even fed with rum for a week in advance. And since it was made without icing, I made a very fancy box that looked like a decorated top hat with a ribbon on it. For Florence I made a beaded bracelet and I painted a picture of Benny the horse for Munroe. They both were very pleased with the gifts.

 It turned out to be the best Christmas ever, but that night when I went to bed I wondered what Mama, Bill, and Kenny were doing. Was it as good a Christmas for them? When would be back together again?

Where Is Home?

For the next three years, I grew more and more settled into Aunt Netty's home and life. I began to think of it as *my* home, while memories of my family and Watertown slipped further into the past. The kids from school became year-round buddies, swimming in the summer, sledding and skating in the winter, and battling a parade of teachers during the school year.

Each spring, I was promoted and soon left Miss Blodgett behind. My new teacher became Miss Atkinson, Aunt Netty's good friend. I liked school a lot better with her.

I grew fonder of Netty as the years went by. I especially enjoyed the ease and pleasures of her life. It made the struggles of Mama, her Bleiler relatives, and my brother Bill's hardscrabble farm stories less appealing. Mama's letters kept postponing her raises, promotions, and the search for a bigger apartment, while Netty bought a shiny new Maxwell auto and pretty dresses for me.

As time went by, I also became interested in the way she dealt with Florence and Munroe. At first I thought she didn't trust them.

Every Monday morning she sat with Florence in the kitchen to work out the menus for the week's meals and discuss whether there were any parties planned or guests coming for dinner. Then later that day or the next, Florence and Munroe would go down to the market to do the shopping. Sometimes, when I was out of school I went with them. We would go to the green grocer's, stop to see Mr. Sabatini for dry goods, Mr. Schiller the butcher, and of course Mr. Boudreaux, the fish monger, who was Billy's father. But Florence never paid for these groceries at that time. She never said so, but I got the feeling she resented that setup.

The bills were paid on Saturday by Aunt Netty. Munroe took Netty downtown on Saturday morning to make the rounds paying each of the merchants in cash. I always liked going with her on Saturdays because often the store owners had a little treat for me. They liked to see Netty coming in. I asked her about this two-step process because it was so different from the way my Mama shopped.

Netty said, "I don't have time to do the shopping, but I also want to thank the merchants for the good service they give us, and I want them to know who pays the bills so they will continue to give us the best service possible. It's not that I don't trust Florence."

I almost never heard her speak sharply to Florence, except once when the beds weren't made up properly for some overnight guests. She just had some harsh words with her and then went about her own business. I thought that was the way everyone spoke to their hired help. Florence just made a bad face behind Netty's back and carried on. But I noticed she didn't ask me to help her make the beds any more.

Sometimes I felt a little guilty about the things Netty and her friends bought for me. But when Margie and Lenore admired them at school, it didn't bother me as much. At times like that I wondered what kinds of dresses and things Mama would be able to afford in New York. I didn't like the idea of being poor again. I remembered the days when we had to move in with Old Aunt Lizzie on School Street.

I sometimes talked with Munroe about these worries. He had been really poor, and wasn't afraid to tell me about it. He often said that the best people he knew were the poor working folks. They seemed to know how to help each other. The rich people he met were often too busy. "Of course, except Mrs. Cross," he always added. "Sunny, she is a mighty fine lady. She learned something special from all those books she reads."

Netty's connections to the literary world and important friends in town and church opened paths to the future I had only dreamed about. And I even got to enjoy her daily reading of poetry at every dinner. On the other hand, my friendship with Munroe grew stronger as his salty ways reminded me of my own Papa. He helped to keep alive the ties to my real family. He always cajoled me into reading to him every letter received from Mama or Bill, and he always insisted that I write a newsy letter in response. He often said, "No matter where a wind takes you, no matter how fancy the town, you always long for your home port. That's the place you dream of dropping your anchor."

Then several things happened in quick succession that forced some big questions on me.

The spring when I turned 14, I got ready to graduate from 8th Grade. One day, Netty asked if I'd like to take a drive in her new Maxwell auto to Exeter, a near-by town. She asked Florence to pack a lunch for us, and while she changed her clothes and got ready to go, I helped make the sandwiches.

While we worked in the kitchen Florence said, "Going to Exeter, eh? I'll bet she's gonna show you that fancy school up there. You stay around here long enough and she'll turn you into an uppity woman just like her and her friends. She treats me like a dummy and threatens to fire me if I don't act smarter. Mark my words, another year or so and there won't be much of the old Clara left."

I started to ask Florence what she meant, but about that time Netty came downstairs and we were ready to go.

I always enjoyed riding in the Maxwell, and she enjoyed demonstrating her skill at the wheel, so we didn't talk much as we rode along. It was a beautiful spring day, so we just enjoyed the ride. Soon, through the woods we saw what looked like an elegant old country estate. When we pulled up to the entrance I saw the sign "Miss Bradbury's School." Aunt Netty said, "I thought you might like to visit here. It's a fine old all-girls school founded years ago. Some of my friends went there before they attended college. Emily Atkinson, your teacher, was one of them. It has a wonderful reputation, and it takes girls your age."

A man met us at the door, and parked the car while Miss Bradbury greeted us and guided us around the school's facilities while introducing us to some of the teachers and students. It looked very exciting and glamorous to me. Miss Bradbury regularly emphasized that my four years here at the Bradbury School aimed at preparing girls for college. That made my head spin.

College. That wasn't something my friends at school talked much about. The boys spoke about getting a job after high school, in their father's store, or on the fishing boats, or maybe a job on the railroad. And the girls dreamed about getting married like their older sisters. But college! I wondered what that would lead to, being a schoolteacher like Miss Atkinson or a librarian like Mrs. Greenleaf? I admired and liked Miss Atkinson a great deal. But would college mean being away from home even longer? Would I ever get to see my family again?

On the way home I began to wonder how this fit in with going back to my family and moving to New York. I asked, "What will Mama think about that school, and who will pay for it? I heard Miss Bradbury speaking about how much she charges."

She said, "Well, Clara, we are just exploring ideas right now. I'm sure that Captain Cross would help pay the bills. He's very fond of you. We'll see how things work out. Do you think you'd enjoy going to school there? You know the kind of education at Miss Bradbury's could lead you to many advantages you couldn't get any other way. You would make friends and contacts there that affect your entire life after. You could leave that life of a butcher's daughter behind. Did you like Miss Bradbury's school?"

"The school looked very nice, but isn't that a boarding school? The girls all seemed to live there."

"Yes, all the girls do live there. In part because many of them come from homes that are far away. That is one of the great advantages of a boarding school. You get to meet girls from very different backgrounds. At a place like Miss Bradbury's they say you learn as much from the other students as from the teachers. Your classmates become life-long friends."

All the way home, I kept trying to imagine what it would be like to go to a live-in boarding school like Miss Bradbury's. It was hard to dream myself into such a place.

By coincidence, the very next day I received another letter from Mama in New York. She had just gotten a raise and had started looking for a bigger place, big enough for all of us ,Bill, Kenny, and me too. Her letter sounded excited and cheerful. Her job had changed again. She now helped the design department by doing sketches of the new styles shown at the big fashion shows in New York. When I read the letter to Munroe and told him about our visit to Miss Bradbury's School, he got very quiet. Unusually quiet. I wondered what he was thinking. Then he said, "Sunny, that's very good news from your Ma, but like lots of favorable breezes, watch out when the wind shifts. Did you know that The Bradbury School is a boarding school? That means all the girls live at the school, not at home?"

"Yes, they told us that. We saw the rooms and the dormitories the girls lived in. There is kind of a housemother for each dormitory. The girls live there all year. That means I'd only get to see Aunt Netty and you on holidays? And when would I get to see Mama or my brothers?"

"Aye, Sunny," he said with a sigh. "That would hurt. Them boarding schools can be painful and expensive, but they get you a mighty fine education. If Mrs. Cross wants to send you there, that would be powerful fine gift. I'd think it over right carefully. Chances like that don't come sailing by every day. But neither do smart, hard-working folks like your Ma. You are the only one who can decide. And I have no doubt that when the time comes, the decision you make will be the right one. I have faith in you, Sunny. A preacher I knew once told me, 'People do not pick figs from thorn bushes, nor grapes from briers.' A good woman brings good things out of the good stored up in her heart. Your Mama stored up many good things in her heart that will flow from you when the time comes. Education like that moves you up into a whole new class and lifestyle."

"Is that what Florence meant? She said that before long Netty would turn me into an 'uppity woman' just like she and her friends were?"

"Well, I'm not sure what Florence meant, but if she's scoffing at education like Mrs. Cross has, I wouldn't pay her much attention. Florence might be a mite different person herself with a bit more schooling. Not saying she's bad, just different. Look how far old Captain Cross got and he don't have much more schooling than eighth grade. Or look at your Ma and Pa. But think how far smart people *with* a good education can go. No sayin' how far. So think it over careful-like, Sunny."

So think it over I did. The more I thought about studying writing and poetry at Miss Bradbury's, the more I liked the idea. I liked how Netty tried to be independent and didn't mind being a little different. I liked the life she led, and I dreamt about her prosperity. What could Mama and my family of cattlemen and butchers do to compare with that? If I ever had a chance of living in a lovely house like Netty's and going to a boarding school at Captain Cross' expense, staying here with Netty seemed the most likely route.

Munroe seemed to be steering me in that direction too. I made my mind up. I decided I would talk to Netty the next morning and tell her how I felt. But before I could, several things happened that changed everything.

One afternoon, when I came out of school, Captain Cross' car was parked out front. He waved to me and asked if I'd like a ride home. I hopped in, but we didn't start up the hill toward High Street and home. Instead he headed down toward the waterfront and his boat yard. Then he turned to me and said, " I understand you and Netty drove up to Exeter a while back. You know, I didn't go to Miss Bradbury's School. In fact I didn't get as much schooling as you've had already. I just learned the boat building trade from my father and grandfather by going to work right here. I don't hold with a lot of book learning and fancy poetry stuff Netty seems to favor. She's steering you in ways I wouldn't go. If I was you, I'd head back to your Mom and get a job-o-work in New York like her. In fact, if you did that, I'd help you get started. I think that might be better for all of us."

I was shocked. What did he mean, "better for all of us" I thought he liked me, and Netty thought he wanted me to stay on and go to Miss Bradbury' school. I thought I was about to cry. I wanted to say, "Why do want to send me away?" But I was afraid to speak to him that way.

Then, when he saw the look on my face he said, "Clara, don't misunderstand me. I do like you, and Netty loves you very much. But that's part of the problem."

I thought, "What problem?" As I started to cry, he looked flustered, started the car and took me home, without saying another word.

That evening at supper, I felt very alone. I wanted to talk to Netty about all this, but was afraid to. I decided to think about it all overnight and tell her in the morning how I felt. But I got off to school before she had finished her bath.

That afternoon, after school, Florence met me at the door and asked me to come with her to her room at the back of the house. I had never been in her room before. She said, "Clara, you and I have always been friends, haven't we? We're kind of alike, you and me. We're from the same side of the tracks, ain't we and we need to stick together."

There is something I'd like to show you. It's kind of a secret. It's something I think you ought to know.

"Do you know that locked room upstairs? Know what's in there?"

"No. I've always wondered."

"Come, I'll show you. She'll probably fire me, but I think it's time you learned." She then took a key from a hook by the door and led me up the front stairs to the second floor. At the top of the stairs, at the front of the house, stood that always-locked door. She used the key to open that special door and we stepped into the dimly lit room. Through the ragged curtains I could make out a dusty old fully made bed and a small child's desk and chair near the window. As my eyes grew accustomed to the gloom, we stepped further into the room leaving footprints on the dusty floor. I saw a bookcase filled with books, while spread on the bed laid a small, white, child's dress now grey with dust. Florence said, "Know who used to belong to this room? It was Miss Lucy's room. Lucy was Mrs. Cross' daughter. Lucy died about 15 years ago, before I got here, and this room ain't been opened since. It's been her little secret all these years. Not many in town know about it or talk about it. She and the Captain have been plotting. I think she and Captain Cross are hoping you will be the new Miss Lucy. She'd kill me if she knew I brought you here."

Later that day, when Netty came home from the library, she went upstairs to her room. When she came down her face was very red and she said, "Did Florence take you into that locked room, Lucy's room? I saw the footprints in front of the door. Did you ask her about that room?"

I said, "No, Ma'am. I didn't."

Netty didn't say anything more right away. She was red in the face and her lips were squeezed tight. She was madder than I had ever seen her. She quietly said, "Go out and ask Munroe to come in and meet me in the library, please. Then please go to your room until dinner." When Munroe came hobbling in, she took both Florence and him into the library. From my room I couldn't hear but when I came down, Florence was nowhere to be seen and there was a racket in the kitchen as Netty was making supper. She said, "I asked Florence to go to her room. I was very angry. She hurt me very much. She brought back painful memories, when she told you about Lucy. It was something I've tried to keep secret, tried to forget for a long time."

I could see how mad she was. Her eyes were still red from crying. She said, "I had told them both no one was to go into that room, ever!"

"Are Florence and Munroe leaving? Did you fire them?"

"No, Munroe convinced me that he wasn't involved, and I told Florence I wanted to think for a while about what happened."

It was a very quiet supper, with no poetry afterward. I was a little surprised that she had not found an appropriate poem to express her anger and hurt. But the only sound was the ticking of the big clock.

The next day was Saturday, the day we usually went downtown to pay for the groceries. Netty was fixing breakfast. Just as I came down the stairs, I could hear her talking with Munroe. He left as I entered the kitchen. As he left, I said to Netty, "I hope I didn't do anything wrong yesterday. I was very frightened."

"No, you've done nothing wrong. I'm sorry I was so angry and short with you. I want to give Florence a second chance. What she did was a terrible shock. It brought back a lot of pain. I'm afraid I lost my temper. It's something I should have told you about long ago. I should not have closed that room. It did no good. It didn't help me get over losing my daughter or my husband."

Then she handed me an old photograph she had brought downstairs. It showed a woman holding a small baby in her arms. The woman was Netty, much younger. "I should have shown you this picture a long time ago. You know you are about the age Lucy would be now. Having you come into my life has been a great joy to me. We are all very fond of you. I think Florence knew that, just as Munroe knew that."

As I passed the photo back to her I said, "Is that Lucy?" She nodded and then replied, "You are so much what I have always dreamed Lucy would be like. I have been thinking for some time about asking your mother about you staying on with me. Just recently I have written her a letter. What do you think? Would you like that?"

"I've been thinking about that too. I think I'd like going to that school we saw. I'd like that very much. I love it here. You have been very good to me, even though I am not your daughter. But Captain Cross wants me to leave. He thinks I am part of the problem. Doesn't he like me? And what did my mother say about my staying on?"

Netty said, "Don't worry about Captain Cross. I will take care of him. He does like you, just as much as I do. I know what his concerns are. As to your mother, I haven't heard from her yet, but when I do, I'm going to suggest she take a couple days off and make a trip here to see you, so we could all talk about it. I told her that Captain Cross and I would be happy to pay for her train fare."

Now, that was news! Maybe Mama would be coming for a visit. I was certainly excited at that thought. But I began to worry about how she would fit in with Aunt Netty's fancy house and elegant friends. Would she look shabby by comparison? How would that make me feel? Then that made me think about clothes. I wondered what Mama would wear, and I wondered whether she would get along with Captain Cross any better than I did.

I worried about that for a few days and then talked it over with Munroe. I said, "Is Netty going to fire Florence? She was madder than I ever saw her. Did you know about Lucy and that room?"

"Yes, I knew about Lucy. Mrs. Cross was badly broken up by Lucy's death. She contracted diphtheria. It took her very quickly, and it happened so soon after she lost her husband. Captain Cross did what he could to help her through her suffering."

"That must have been awful for her. It makes my worries seem small. But I am worried. I'm a little worried about Mama coming here. After all, I haven't seen her in almost four years. Will I even recognize her? Will she recognize me?"

As usual, he had some words of wisdom that calmed me down. He said, "Don't worry about Florence or Mrs. Cross. I spoke to Mrs. Cross about Florence. I think she has been forgiven. And Mrs. Cross is a very strong lady. She rode out that storm years ago, and your presence here has been a big help. As for your Ma, you ought to have more faith. Once I shipped out on a New Bedford whaler. We went around The Horn and didn't come back to these shores for nigh onto four years. But as soon as I saw the lighthouse at the mouth of the old Merrimack River it felt like I'd never been away. The eyes never forget home waters and your own folks. It will be the same with you and your Ma."

Mama Comes to Visit

A few days later, a letter came to Netty from New York.
Mama said she'd get to Newburyport on Saturday, June 10.
That turned out to be the day after my school ended for the
season. Perfect! But that was only 2-3 weeks away!

I could hardly wait. I wanted to make a good impression, and
I think Netty wanted to do so too. She even asked me what
kind of poetry I thought Mama would like to hear after
dinner. I told about the stories my Papa used to tell Billy and
me about the Wild West. Maybe she could find poems like
that.

There seemed to be so much to get ready. We all pitched in
to help. Netty began planning a party to introduce Mama to
her friends, and that of course meant cleaning, shopping and
cooking. Netty and Captain Cross met several times at our
house for long evening discussions that piqued my curiosity.
But not even Munroe could find out what those were about.

In the weeks before she arrived, I worried a lot about Mama.
Had she changed? How much had I changed? Would she
recognize me? After all, I was four years older. Would she
still want me? What would Mama think if I told her I was
thinking of staying on with Netty? After living by herself in
New York for so long maybe she would be happy to have
me stay. Then I worried about how she would fit in with
Netty's friends. They always looked so stylish and well

dressed. Would Mama seem like a hick, a simple factory worker?

The closer we got to June 10, the queasier I became. I think Netty sensed how troubled I was, but I talked more to Munroe than to Netty about my worries. Netty read light and cheerful poems every evening after supper, but that didn't help. And not even Munroe could make me feel better, though he tried. There just seemed to be too much to think through.

I liked living with Aunt Netty and I guess I loved her very much. She had certainly done many good things for me. But somehow I missed my family and Mama. Staying with Netty seemed like abandoning them; like running away. When I first got here I was angry and frightened at being sent away. I resented being forced away from my family. But that was long ago. I was older now and it didn't hurt so much. I had learned how hard it would have been for Mama, if in addition to working, she had to take care of all three of us too. But I did like the idea of going to Miss Bradbury's School and maybe to college.

I didn't sleep very much on that Friday night. Even though her train wasn't due until the afternoon of the 10th, I got up early. Netty kept me busy picking flowers from the garden and setting them around the house. And I remember she twice had me ask Munroe to go to the train station to double check when the train from Boston came on Saturdays. Late in the afternoon Captain Cross came to wait at our house.

Finally, as the big clock in the dining room struck 6:00, Munroe came back from the station with her. When she came through the front door into the hallway everything changed. She rushed to me with arms open saying, "Sissy, Sissy, liebchen," as we both choked on our tears.

As we hugged and cried all my worries washed away. I didn't have to worry about recognizing her; she looked wonderful . . . just like that morning in Hay Market Square four years before.

It took a while before I realized it, but Netty and Captain Cross had been standing there watching our happy scene. I guess there were polite introductions, but I clung to Mama happily, drying my tears and not seeing much else. I think it was a few minutes before I realized it, but Netty was crying too. Only much later did she tell me that it looked like the reunion she and Lucy would never have.

Munroe had brought Mama's bags into the hallway. I helped her carry them up the stairway to one of the spare bedrooms. While she unpacked, we babbled on about her trip, New York, her new apartment, about Bill and Kenny, and about the many people we knew in Watertown. It was almost as if we hadn't been apart all these years. I talked about Mr. Munroe, my school friends and that Netty had taken me to visit Miss Bradbury's boarding school. She asked what I thought about that and I said that I wanted very much to go there. She winced and said, "Well, we'll see'. But we didn't talk more about it then.

That evening, as the house filled up with Netty's friends. I began to feel very proud and happy. Proud that I lived there and knew all these wonderful people. I was happy that Mama fit in so well with them. For the first time, the ladies of Newburyport looked just a little out of fashion next to my Mama. She wore a light blue afternoon gown made of silk and flowered chiffon with long transparent sleeves. The skirt stopped well above her ankles and she wore beautiful pointed, high heeled shoes that matched her dress.

Netty's friends admired her stylish clothes, but also spoke with fascination of her independence, skill, and courage in the aggressive New York fashion industry. I felt very proud and stood next to her as often as I could. It was a little embarrassing when Netty and her friends said so many nice things about me, and the way I had grown up during the few years. I think I blushed at the comments Miss Atkinson made about how well I had done in school. She added that she hoped I would go on with my schooling, but no one mentioned Miss Bradbury's school

After dinner, as she always did, Netty read some poetry. Actually, this time she didn't really read it because she knew it well enough to recite the piece by heart. We had read it together several times before. It was called, "Luck" by her friend Abbie Farwell Brown:

I sought a four-leaved clover, -
The grass was gemmed with dew, -
I searched the meadow over;
To find a four-leaved clover;
I was a lucky rover, -
You sought the charm-grass, too,
And seeking luck and clover
I found it – finding you.

At the last line, she looked right at me and of course I cried.

The next morning Captain Cross came back again in his fancy car. We all met in the library, and while Florence served tea, the Captain started by saying, "Mrs. Smyth, we have grown very fond of your daughter, Clara. Over the time she has been with us she has proven to be a bright and cheerful child, and she has been a great joy to us all, which is why many people here call her 'Sunny.' She has been a unique source of happiness to my daughter-in-law. As you may know, Netty lost a daughter of her own some years ago. Your daughter has helped to fill that void. Netty has proposed that we let Sunny stay on with us. I know you want the best for your daughter. She deserves a good education. So we have investigated a nearby private school for her and would undertake to pay the expense of her attendance. We might even consider adopting her, but felt it was only proper to discuss these ideas with you in person."

Stunned, I said to myself, "Adoption! No one mentioned anything about adoption. I'm not an orphan. I already have a family." This made me very angry and nervous. That would make everything different.

At this point, Mama started to say, "Captain Cross, that is very kind of you . . ." when Netty interrupted her by saying, "Caleb, I have changed my mind." Then she turned to me and said, "Clara, you know I love you as dearly as my own daughter, and have instigated this idea more than anyone. I'd love to have you stay on and live with me. But yesterday when I watched how you greeted your mother, I realized how wrong that would be. It is not for me to try to fill the void in my heart left by the loss of Lucy by creating a hole in someone else's heart. Your dear mother has been without you for too long. I have no wish to extend that any longer."

At that point Mama turned to me and said, "Clara, I think you should have a say in this matter. I know you have loved living here with Netty, and I know you would like to go to the private school she has in mind. But I think you and I ought to take a little time to talk this over by ourselves. Captain Cross, may we get back to you later on with our thoughts?"

So Mama and I went for a walk in the garden. As we stepped into the sunshine, we passed by the old lilac bushes by the back door. Their blooms made the whole garden smell wonderful. Mama said, "What lovely lilacs! That's the one thing I miss about New York. Where I live now there is no garden. That's the one thing I want when we move."

"Sissy, I really like Netty. She has done a wonderful thing for us keeping you all these years since Papa died. But if that old sea dog thought he could buy us off the way he bought that fancy car, he badly misjudged me. Consider adopting you! – Ha! I'm glad Netty cut him off when she did or I might have said something I'd regret. I will always be grateful for all that Netty has done for you and for me, but I won't let his money buy his way into our family. What do you think? Let's talk about Captain Cross' proposal."

In the past, this is the kind of situation where I had often turned to Munroe for help. But I could see that this time what I felt was more important. I remembered how badly I felt the time Captain Cross had tried to talk his way around me, and also how good it felt when I saw Mama come through that door yesterday. I would always be grateful to Netty. She had taught me I didn't need to depend on Munroe or anyone.

"Mama, last night I said that I'd like to go to that boarding school and live with Netty some more. She has been very good to me and taught me many things. But I don't want to be adopted. This isn't my home. As much as I like it here, I want to be with you. I could never be her Lucy, or even her Clara. I just want to be 'Sissy' like I was before. So when can I move to New York with you? Can we find a place with lilacs? Just like these?"

And just then, who should come limping out of the barn, but Munroe. He carried a hoe and seemed to be heading for his flowerbeds.

He said, "Good morning, Mrs. Smyth, and top-o-the-morning to you, Sunny."

"Well, Mr. Munroe, it is nice to meet you. Sissy has told me a lot about you. She tells me you have given her plenty of fatherly help and guidance. I'm grateful to you for that. We have just had a conversation with Captain Cross that left us both quite upset. He made a proposal for adoption that I think put Sissy in a very difficult position, both with Netty and with me. Have you ever heard talk of Netty or the Captain adopting Sissy?"

"No Ma'am, I haven't. But that doesn't surprise me. Captain Cross is a very proud man, but I think he might be a difficult relative."

"I think Sissy, Sunny, recognized that. I think your good advice has given her wisdom beyond her years. I think she has decided that she may be leaving here soon, but when she does she will be a stronger and more independent person because of your guidance."

"So, Sunny you will be leaving us soon? Though I think that is right and proper, it will make us all a lot sadder. Mrs. Smyth, your sweet daughter here has been a right fine joy to us, especially to this old salt."

When we returned to the library, Mama carried a branch of lilacs from the garden. She said, "Captain Cross, you have proposed an attractive but life-changing idea. I don't think I fully realized how much I missed my daughter until we smelled these lovely flowers from the garden. Perhaps bringing her back to New York, some of that same joy could be returned to my life. But in fairness to everyone involved, I believe we'd better take a day or so to talk it over. If Netty will keep me as her guest for another day, I would like to discuss it a little more carefully.

"Netty, I will always be deeply grateful for the kindness you have shown to me and to Clara. She was a child when she came to you. Whenever she returns to me, you will be sending back a strong young woman."

So Mama and I spent that evening talking, mostly in the sweet-smelling garden. Sometimes Mama tried to talk me into staying on to continue my education with Netty, but for both of us the stumbling block was adoption. We came to see that Captain Cross wanted to give back to Netty the child she had lost, but would only do so if that child would continue the Cross family name. Neither of us would compromise on that. After that our conversations turned toward New York and how soon I could get there.

So the decision was made, and to this day I believe that lilacs caused it as much as anything.

Together Again

On Monday Mama had to take the morning train back to New York. Munroe took us to the station in the carriage and waited while we said our goodbyes. Even though I knew I would be seeing Mama again in a month or so, this seemed almost like when I left her at the Hay Market Square years ago. She said, "Sissy, I'm so proud of you. You are a beautiful young lady. I sorry Papa isn't here to see you." As usual, that made me cry. She dug out her handkerchief to dry my eyes as the conductor began shouting "All Aboard." Climbing onto the train, I watched as she found a seat by a window and blew a kiss. I could see that her eyes were wet, too. I stood sobbing and waving to her until the train pulled out. New York seemed a long way away to me just then.

The next weeks went slowly, although Netty filled them as best she could. In late June, when the weather got warmer, she took my school friends, Margie and Lenore, and me to Plum Island Beach for a picnic. We all rode in her Maxwell and giggled the whole way. We wore our bathing suits, but the water was too cold for real swimming. We just waded in the water and splashed each other. Even so, we all had a wonderful outing.

Over the Fourth of July weekend, Netty had a big garden party. She invited all her friends and even some of my friends from school. It was a wonderful way for me to see them all one more time. In some ways it made me sad, because I liked many of these people so much. Margie and her mom from Seligmann's had become good friends. Miss Atkinson, my teacher and Miss Greenleaf, the librarian, had all been very good to me. I would miss them all.

Then a letter came from Mama saying that she had found a nice apartment in a two-family house in the Inwood section of northern Manhattan. She would move in on August first and suggested that I plan to be there over the following weekend. She had made arrangements for her sister, Aunt Elsie, to meet me in Boston at North Station and see to it that Bill, Kenny and me got to the right train for New York at South Station. It would be a long trip, but we would all travel together. She even included some money to pay for my ticket to Boston.

So that set the date, a little over two weeks away. In that time I had to say goodbye to the place I had called home for several years of my life, and store up memories of all that had happened here. In the evenings, at suppertime, as Netty read poems or stories, my mind, wandered as I thought about places and people that had meant so much to me over the years. I couldn't help but wonder what it might have been like if I had let myself become Netty's Lucy. Would life had been more fun going to Miss Bradbury's? But there was no time for dreaming and guesswork. I had to get ready to move onward to New York.

One evening, when I sat down at the dinner table, there were two nicely wrapped packages by my plate. They were from Netty with a note that said, "For my dear Clara." The first one I opened held three small books: one was a signed copy of a book by Abbie Farwell Brown entitled *John of the Woods*; one was a copy of Jane Austen's *Pride and Prejudice*; and the third was *Jane Eyre* by Charlotte Brontë.

Netty said, "I hope you will like them. They are all books that affected me deeply in very different ways."

The second package was a box of stationery printed with my name. She said, "I hope you will write to me often, and not forget the time we had together. It has meant a lot to me." As I rushed to the other side of the table to give her a big hug, she said, "I hope you will always live up to your potential. Hitch your wagon to a star."

That night, as I lay in bed reading, I began to wonder what she meant. Was she the kind of "star" I should hook my wagon to? Or was she only saying, "Aim for the stars"? Sometimes she spoke in riddles, but she always made me think.

The next day, for one of the last times, I went out to the barn to talk with Munroe. Perhaps he would help me unravel some of the riddles. I told him about the books she had given me and what she has said. He said, "Well, she is a literary lady, but I don't reckon she is suggesting you become a lady writer like her friend. But I'm a mind that she is telling you to set your sights way over the top of the mizzen topsails and learn from the best writers around, the way she did. Sounds like mighty good advice to me."

"And like Mrs. Cross, I think you will go far, but I can't give you books to guide your way. But I figured you might need to get your bearings now and again, so I dug out this old compass of mine. I had it rerigged so's whenever you need, it will always point to me. I hope you won't ever forget this old sailor, for I'll ne'er forget my Sunny."

There must have been a huggin' bug going around, because I gave Munroe the biggest hug yet.

I stayed with Aunt Netty for another week or so while Mama found and moved into the apartment in Inwood. She found an apartment in a two-family house not far from Fort Tryon Park and close to the subway line that took her downtown to her work. The apartment had three cheerful bedrooms, and there was even a small garden where we could plant some lilacs.

So during the August of 1917 Ken, Bill and I moved into New York. The Bleilers met us at South Station in Boston and saw us onto the train. It was a long train ride, but the family would be together again. But when we got to New York, Bill made an announcement that shook us all up. He wanted to join the American Expeditionary Force in France, and planned on enlisting in the Army. Mama could not talk him out of it. We would soon be separated once again!

Before I left Newburyport, Abbie Farwell Brown did come to town on a speaking tour and I got to meet her. I still have her book as well as the Jane Austen and Charlotte Brontë books Netty gave me. In later years Netty became the head of the Newburyport Library Foundation, and one of its greatest benefactors.

Netty wrote to me often, and though she never married again, she often thought of me and introduced me as her daughter when I visited. In 1936, I came Newburyport with my young son. We enjoyed seeing the beautiful old house on High Street and some my old friends, Margie, Lenore, and Bill. We laughed about our days with Miss Blodgett. We compared notes on the "old days" before the war, and then I told them about my Bohemian life in Greenwich Village and my trip to Santiago, Chile to get married. Those things would never have happened without the wisdom and balance of Monroe, and the generosity of Aunt Netty, the lady who lost a daughter, twice.

CPSIA information can be obtained
at www.ICGtesting.com
Printed in the USA
JSHW050851150721
16785JS00006BA/136